Michael M. Dediu

To pour PEACE
from a cup full of arms,
MELT ALL ARMS!

Moving from arms race, to
peace enjoyment

DERC Publishing House
Nashua, New Hampshire, U. S. A.

Copyright ©2021   by Michael M. Dediu

Published and printed in the
United States of America
On the Great Seal of the United States are included:
E Pluribus Unum (Out of many, one)
Annuit Coeptis (He has approved of the undertakings)
Novus Ordo Seclorum (New order of the ages)

Library of Congress Control Number: 2021905075

Dediu, Michael M.

To pour Peace from a cup full of arms, MELT ALL ARMS!
Moving from arms race, to enjoying peace

ISBN-13: 978-1-950999-34-7

MSG0593871_7szEN7lw6s04BX86i12j

1-10262155831
1-4PPTM5E
26RHN7IE
04497D

Preface

It is well known now that the old war-oriented "Si vis pacem, para bellum" ("If you want peace, prepare for war") was replaced for good with "Si vis pacem, para PACEM!" ("If you want peace, prepare for PEACE!"). People cannot accept the fact that the arms continue to outnumber the books – people ask for zero arms!

Now comes the question: how in the world can you pour peace from a cup (our planet Terra!) full to the brim with arms?!
Very simple – just melt all the arms!

The more preparations for war, the more unhappiness for people.

This book provides simple and clear ideas, which will bring peace, no arms, freedom, good health, good education, good jobs, harmony and prosperity for all.

No arms = peace + better life.

Michael M. Dediu, Ph. D.

Nashua, New Hampshire, U. S. A., 12 March 2021

New York in 2007: West 42nd Street near 7th Avenue and Times Square, with many tall buildings around, like the Conde Nast Building (1996-1999, 264 m, 48-story office tower, on the left).

Table of Contents

1 – World is a big family of over 7.7 billions of people

All people on the planet are scared stiff of these daily preparations for war – they all want to quickly change to preparing for peace.

Socrates: "The secret of change is to focus all your energy, not on fighting the old, but on building the new." – exactly this we are doing. The shortest route to growth and prosperity for all is to have peace, freedom, good health, good education, good jobs, good science & technology, and harmony.

The big family, of over 7.7 billions of people, wants peace.

When the people will have a friendly, helpful, fast, polite, modest and very smart world management, it will be easy to maintain peace.

But until then what do we do?

Because right now the situation is really bad: the world is facing serious threats and challenges. There are many uncertainty factors.

The military technology is developing rapidly, while competition and rivalry are growing stronger and morphing into new forms.

There are old smoldering conflicts in various regions of the planet, and new ones keep appearing.

The leading countries are actively developing their offensive weapons.

The nuclear club is receiving new members. The NATO infrastructure is expanding.

There are efforts to militarize outer space.

There is broad use of artificial intelligence in creating military arms, in particular reconnaissance and attack unmanned aerial vehicles, laser and hypersonic systems, and weapons based on new principles of physics, as well as robotic systems capable of performing a variety of tasks on the battlefield, just to kill more people!

Many prepare for war day and night!

But soon, with the new World Constitution, the things will change:

Advisors (and all the others) cannot declare war, reprisals or capture land or water.

Advisors (and all the others) cannot raise and support armies, navy, or any military forces.

Paris in 2013: L'Opéra de Paris (or l'Académie Nationale de Musique, or l'Opéra Garnier, or le Palais Garnier, or l'Opéra), a 1,979-seat opera house, 1861-1875, now mainly used for ballet.

The west side of Tokyo Skytree seen from the stairs coming from Tokyo Skytree Station on Tobu Skytree Line. The broadcasting, restaurant, and observation tower is located in Sumida, 5 km northeast of the Imperial Palace. 634 m in March 2011, making it the tallest tower in the world, and the second tallest structure in the world. Without antenna it is 495 m, top observation floor is at 451.2 m, and the second observation floor is at 350 m. It has 13 elevators. The exterior lattice is painted a color called "Skytree White". The tower is illuminated using LED lights.

Start discussions

The first step is to start talking at different levels.

What would it be the best level to start with?

Military – they will be the first to die if something bad happens, therefore they should begin to discuss to change the current enemies into friends.

Instead of building very dangerous arms to destroy each other, and millions of people around them, better start building beautiful houses for them, for their families, their friends, and for others, with the budgets they already have.

Paris in 2013: Place de la Concorde (1772): The Egyptian obelisk (Ramses the Great, 1250 BC, 23 m), Marine Nationale (1758, left).

Change school history books

Instead of telling kids all the terrible wars each country had all the time, tell them of the beautiful peace which existed between the wars, in which time, by the way, all the important things on Earth happened.

This is long overdue.

If You Want Peace, Prepare for Peace! – this is a well-known book (please see Bibliography). Also, If You Want Peace, Study Peace! All people applaud Colleges which are turning against the history of military conflict, because by studying peace students will be prepared for peace, while the wars will be mentioned as a very bad part of the history, not to be forgotten, and never to be repeated. Studying war, brings war – studying peace, brings peace.

Venezia in 2012: Piazza San Marco, the west façade of Basilica di San Marco, with its great arches and marble decorations, is in the back, il Campanile (the Bell Tower) on the right

Begin to visit each other more frequently

The people should be visiting each other frequently – many times, just using computers and phones for video friendly discussions, would be a great progress.

And make friends everywhere.

Japan: the north side of Mount Fuji (3,776 m) seen from Kawaguchi city, near Kawaguchiko (Lake Kawaguchi, down right), 100 km south-west of Tokyo, 17 km north of Mount Fuji

2- Levels of World Peaceful Collaboration

There should be several levels of establishing peaceful cooperation:
- family
- school
- university
- company
- city
- counties
- provinces or regions (states in the U.S)
- country
- United Nations

Boston Harbor (1614): Rowes Wharf (1666, 1764, 1987): the stern (rear) of Clipper Stad Amsterdam (2000, 76 m x 10.5 m x 4.8 m x 46.5 m) moored here, with the poop deck clearly visible.

Family Peaceful Collaboration

There are around 3 billions of families (including also the singles as a temporary family of one person).

Each family should be in peaceful collaboration with at least 3 other families from 3 different countries.

They should maintain contact by e-mails, phone, mails and visits. The family is the foundation of the society on Earth. It is at home, in the lap of the family, that we receive the basics of our worldview, develop our personal qualities, and absorb practical, cultural and spiritual ideals. It is very important to bring up the younger generation in the spirit and on the values of a large and close-knit family with many children, where everyone, both children and parents, takes care of each other, and to create conditions for the professional and creative fulfilment of young people, as well as the settlement of essential social and practical problems. The healthcare system must be reliable, and strong support should be given to the pro-natal population policy, young families, mothers, fathers and children.

Because all families need assistance from time to time, and the big 7.7 B family on Earth contains billions of small families, all of them will have the assistance they need – this will be the result of one country well organized and managed.

Roma in 2011: Trajan's column was erected in 113 AD in honor of Emperor Trajan. It is located at the Forum of Trajan, near Piazza Venezia and Altare della Patria. The column commemorates Trajan's victories in Dacia (now Romania), and it is 42 meters tall, including its base.

School Peaceful Collaboration

There are around 1.3 billion enrolled students in primary and secondary schools, but there are many children between 7 and 18 who are not enrolled in schools yet - this is a major issue which must be addressed.

On the planet there are around 3 millions of schools.

Normally each school should be in contact with at least 4 other school from different countries, for peaceful collaboration.

Finland in 2013: Helsinki Central railway station (1907 – 1914), on Brunnsgatan, in the city center.

Move war-related money to educating children

The Governments really need to allocate war-related money to having all school-age kids in schools – it's just a matter of common sense, and it is much cheaper than building some huge destructive arms, and much better for the future.

Sustainable peace can be achieved only by eliminating all arms.

The global arms market will be transformed in the global medical and life-improving market.

Japan, Nikko, (140 km north of Tokyo): Toshogu Shrine, Japan's most lavishly decorated shrine, and the mausoleum of Tokugawa Ieyasu, the founder of the Tokugawa shogunate (1600-1850).

University Peaceful Collaboration

Some universities have already good collaboration with others, but this should be extended and improved – each university to have peaceful collaboration with at least 5 universities from different countries and continents.

They can really establish some high standards of peaceful collaboration, which should be an example for all.

Self-improvement is essential - Marcus Aurelius (26 April 121, Rome, Italy – 17 March 180, (58.9) Vindobona, now in Austria, Roman emperor for 19 years from 161 to 180 and a Stoic philosopher. one of the great rulers of the Roman Empire), sets forth a series of self-reflective essays intended as a guide for his own self-improvement.

Canada: interior of Toronto Pearson International Airport (1984, 22 km northwest of downtown Toronto, in Mississauga, Ontario).

Company Peaceful Collaboration

Companies, and any other type of institutions and organizations, should have extensive peaceful collaboration with others from other countries – it is good for business and for peace.

Also, for beginning, some companies should substitute the production of war devices with peaceful devices, useful for everybody. Some small companies, which are interested in this, are speaking up now, because they are uniquely worried that the current unstable situation will dry up the venture capital funding that drives their industry and, in turn, make it impossible for the small startups, that turn basic research into new products or medicines, to get off the ground.

From Tokyo Skytree (2011, 634 m, at 350 m) looking south-west, Sumida river (right oblique), Edo-Tokyo Museum (center-up white), tall buildings near Tokyo Imperial Palace (up left) and Shinjuku (up right).

City Level Peaceful Collaboration

Many cities are already in contact between them, but this should be generalized: each city should have peaceful collaboration with at least 7 other cities from different countries and continents.

For example, Venice: Venetians woke Wednesday, 13 Nov 2019, to distressing scenes after the highest tide in 50 years washed through the historic Italian city, beaching gondolas, trashing hotels, and sending tourists fleeing through rapidly rising waters. It was an exceptional overnight "Alta Acqua" high tide water level. The extraordinarily intense "acqua alta," or high waters, peaked at 1.87 m. Only once, since records began in 1923, has the water crept even higher, reaching 1.94 m in 1966.

They need a lot of help.

Roma in 2011: Piazza del Colosseo with the Arch of Constantine (315 AD, left), and Amphitheatrum Flavium (Colosseum, 80 AD).

County Level Peaceful Collaboration

Some like the idea, and there is hope that each county (or small district, with a few towns) will have peaceful collaboration with at least 8 counties from the world, in which case the situation will improve fast.

USA, Boston (founded in 1630) in 2009: tall ships from many countries, at the Boston Fish Pier (opened in 1915).

Province Level Peaceful Collaboration

This is an important level, and their commitment to a peaceful collaboration with at least 9 provinces (or states in the U.S.) from different countries and continents would be a great contribution to peace.

Japan: The Symbol Statue "Beautiful and ugly" (beautiful on the left and ugly - right) in Kawaguchiko (Lake Kawaguchi back).

Country Level Peaceful Collaboration

Now we arrived at the most significant level, were, actually, the whole issue can be totally solved.

If, for example, G20 would invite all the countries to join the club and work for peace, the Peaceful Terra would begin to take shape.

All the people of the world will be proud citizens of only one country, called Peaceful Terra, with total area of over 509 M km^2, and land area over 148 M km^2.

Being just one country, there are no borders:

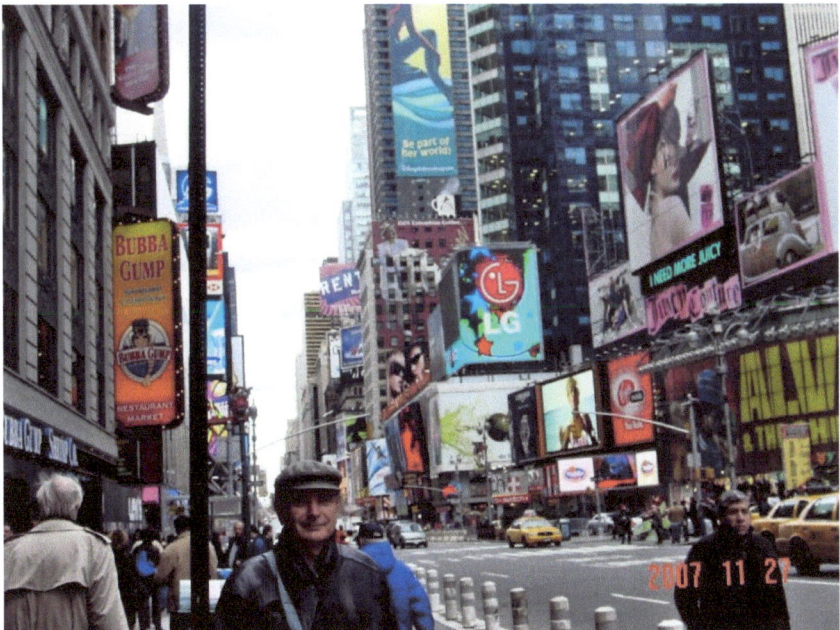

New York (1624) in 2007: on 7th Avenue in Times Square, with the Bertelsmann Building (1990, 223 m, 44 floors, center-right).

Roma in 2011: the south-west side of the Fontana dei Quatro Fiumi, in Piazza Navona. The Fountain of the Four Rivers was designed in 1651 by Gian Lorenzo Bernini (1598-1680). The base of the fountain is a basin which supports four river gods, and above them, an ancient Egyptian obelisk. As a group, they represent four major rivers of the four continents: the Nile representing Africa, the Danube representing Europe, the Ganges representing Asia, and the Río de la Plata representing the Americas.

United Nations Level Peaceful Collaboration

Finally, United Nations, certainly, do many useful peace-related tasks, however something is missing - they need to work at the people level, not only at the government level.

Peace must be built from ground up.

People want:
NOT kill everything with lasers – people want lasers only to make people healthier
NOT space for war – space is for people to enjoy
NOT 5G for war – 5G is for better life
NOT quantum electronic warfare – quantum is for better computers for people

From Tokyo Skytree (2011, 634 m, at 350 m) looking west, Sumida river with bridges Kotoibashi (right) and Tobu Skytree Line and Isesaki Line (left), Asakusa district (after river), Bokutei Dori and Metropolitan Expressway Nr. 6 Mukojima Route (down).

3 – Peaceful Collaboration Management

At each level people will elect a manager to coordinate the work, to keep the financial records and other records.

All this collaboration will create a peaceful atmosphere, which will reduce the risk of war.

There are many useful books on this subject, including "Our Future is Sustainable Peace and Prosperity – Moving from conflicts to harmony and peace", "Our Future Depends on Good World Educations – Moving from frail education to solid education", and "Friendly, Helpful & Smart World Management - Moving from bureaucracy to responsive world management".

Many people in the world suffer from sickness, hunger, unemployment, bureaucratic mismanagement, and isolation, but soon these issues will be solved using the Constitution of the World.

Italy, Rome (753 BC) in 2011: Sapienza – Università di Roma (1303). The Chapel with the inscription "Omnium Artifex Sapientia, Pius XII P.M., 1948.

Small Budget

Some small budgets for peace preparation can very easily be taken from the huge war budgets of the world – total over $1.6 T in 2015, around $215/world-person. The U.S. accounted for 37% of the total, in 2018 it was $639 B, or $1955/US-person. Just 1% of this total war budget would mean $16 B for peace.

A lot of money is wasted on war related things. How many average houses for families could have been built in 2015 with this wasted money? Over 10 M houses for over 30 M people.

All budgets will have surplus of 2% - there will be a strict application of the Latin aphorism: "Sumptus censum ne superset" (Let not your spending exceed your income).

An artificial seawater tank (right) at Sumida Aquarium (on the fifth and sixth floors in the West Zone of Tokyo Skytree Town, 2012).

Finland in 2010: a nice building in the center of Helsinki, on Pohjoisesplanade (left) and Fabannkatu (to the right), with a beautiful park on the left.

Volunteers

Volunteers will be needed, and they are always welcome to join the growing group of people working and preparing for peace.

Japan, Kyoto (678) in 2008: traditional houses near the Nishi Hongan-ji Temple ("Western Temple of the Original Vow", 1602).

Permanent contact with all people

An important aspect of this preparation for peace is the permanent contact with all people - by visiting them, phone calls, e-mails, videos, and mail, to keep everybody calm, friendly and peace oriented.

Then the transfer to a sustainable peace, freedom, good health, good education, good jobs and prosperity will be easy - all the people want exactly this.

The acquiescence of the people to destructive, abusive and arbitrary rules, restrictions, and mandates is not good – the people should calmly and politely explain that these things are not appropriate for a civilized society.

Soon, an electronic world referendum will be organized every three months. The main questions will be:

1. Are you satisfied with the Government?
2. What Government work is good?
3. What Government work is not good?
4: Suggestions for improvement:

Common language and alphabet

When preparing for peace, it will be normal to have a common language and alphabet on Earth.

Because English is a de facto common language now, it will be taken as the basis of the world language, let's call it Mundo, which will be taught in all schools, and used in the world government.

All the other languages will continue as secondary languages.

The same is true for the Latin alphabet, which will be used everywhere, with other alphabets as secondary.

The teachers will have a very significant role in implementing this idea.

Venezia in 2012: Costa Fascinosa cruise ship passing south of Piazza San Marco, and a gondola (right down).

Work for everybody

The beauty is that this preparation for peace gives work to everybody.

If unemployed, this is a temporary job, at world minimum wage, until they find a better job.

And also, for those who don't look for a job – this is a nice and very useful hobby – they will be in contact with many interesting and friendly people.

Taking into account that the 2018 Global Wealth Report from Credit Suisse shows that total global wealth has now reached $317 trillions (circa $41,000/person), just a tiny 0.01% would mean $31.7 B for peace.

And this peace would obviously bring a tri-fold increase in Global Wealth!

Like in any big family, there are differences, because some work more, some spend less, some move faster, and, especially, some are sick – this is the main reason for differences: not all people can be equally sick, some people are sicker than others. However, all the people and the government will work to help each other.

It is a major responsibility of the Government to increase the global wealth, and to train those in need to have better working abilities and opportunities.

There will always be plenty of jobs at world minimum wage (assisting other people, for example), and the standard situation will be this: more jobs than available people, so people will choose the jobs they like the most.

No unemployment, no homelessness, no begging, no tipping – just all working harmoniously, having good houses, and helping each other.

Japan, Kyoto (678) in 2008: the hall gate of the Shinshu Honbyo Temple (1321, until 1987 Higashi Hongan-Ji, total area 99,000 m^2, interior area 29,700 m^2), on the west side of Karasuma Dori, north of Shichijo Dori and south of Hanayacho Dori.

Tax form

At the tax level, it would be very appropriate to have on the last line of the tax form, just before the signature, a very simple question: How much of this tax do you want to go for peaceful purposes?

People need only truth in order to create a long term peaceful and harmonious society.

Cape Inubo, 100 km east of Tokyo, 40 km east of Narita International Airport, from the airplane over Choshi, looking east: Tone River (left), Choshihoncho city on the right bank of Tone River, Chiba Institute of Science (center right), Shin Port (center-left), to the right up Choshi Port, Kashima-nada Sea (up).

Current government buildings and equipment

Some of the current government buildings and equipment should be used for preparation for peace - not all government buildings and equipment are used 100%, therefore there is room for some people preparing for peace.

In Dwight D. Eisenhower's farewell speech, on January 17, 1961, the former famous Five Star General in the Army, Supreme Commander of the Allied Forces in Europe in World War II, and the 34th President of the United States warned of the dangers of allowing a Military-Industrial Complex to take control: "In the councils of government, we must guard against the acquisition of unwarranted influence, whether sought or unsought, by the military–industrial complex". The Military-Industrial Complex is a term that denotes an interdependent relationship between a nation's military, economy, and politics, and it is valid for all nations.

4 - Preparation for Peace Institut

A Preparation for Peace Institut (PPI) will be created - a non-profit organization dedicated to preparation for peace.

There are already some organizations dedicated to peace – they could help to create this PPI.

Washington, D.C. (1790) in 2007, National Gallery of Art (1937, in the National Mall).

Assisting people on peaceful objectives

This PPI will help people on all peace-related tasks.

People will pay much attention to eliminate fraud, waste, abuse and mismanagement in Government.

Japan: the north side of Mount Fuji (3,776 m, 1707 last eruption) seen from Kawaguchiko (Lake Kawaguchi, 6 km^2, 830 m elevation, 100 km south-west of Tokyo, 17 km north of Mount Fuji), with a branch of a blossomed cherry.

No bureaucracy

PPI will help to eliminate bureaucracy as much as possible - firstly, they will set an example themselves, and then help others.

It is a strict requirement for the top management, and for all others, to be highly civilized, polite, courteous, harmonious and efficient.

Who wants to work for the world government must have good manners.

Harmony in the world starts from the harmony and good manners of the people in the world government.

Constant attention will be focused on avoiding duplication at all levels of the world government – there must be continuous collaboration between all levels, to prevent duplication, and to eliminate it, if it was found.

A vice is nourished by being concealed (from Latin: Alitur vitium vivitque tegendo).

Receiving comments from people

PPI will invite comments from people on preparing for peace issues - always there are people with good ideas, and some even with resources to work for peace.

Washington, D.C. (1790) in 2007: National Archives and Records Administration building (1935), on Constitution Avenue.

No violence

Eliminating corruption, organized crime and drug trafficking is helpful for peace - violent activities must be eliminated in order to have peace.

Non-violence is a strict requirement for all activities on Earth.

The first rule for everybody on Earth comes from the Hippocratic Oath: Primum non nocere - first do not harm.

Japan in 2008: the northern side of Kawaguchiko (Lake Kawaguchi, 6 km^2, 830 m elevation), with a splendid statue (left), 17 km north of Mt. Fuji (3,776 m), 100 km south-west of Tokyo.

Tokyo (1150) in 2008: Tokyo Metropolitan Gov. Bldg., 243 m, 48
fl, 1991, in Shinjuku, two observation decks on floor 45, 202 m..

Peace volunteers

Naturally PPI will focus on peace volunteers - they will play a key role in this worldwide preparation for peace.

Kawaguchi city, near Kawaguchiko (Lake Kawaguchi, 6 km2, 830 m elevation), 100 km south-west of Tokyo, 17 km north of Mt Fuji

Harmony

It is important to help people to be friendly and happy, to live in harmony, and PPI will certainly assist - this is the shortest way to achieve a peaceful world.

Vaccine distribution would not have any problems in the one country Peaceful Terra, as described in the Constitution of the World.

Canada, Niagara Falls in 2013: Niagara Sky Wheel in Dinosaur Park and Miniature Golf, near Clifton Hill and Oneida Lane, 1.5 km north of the Horseshoe Falls.

Family assistance

Because everything starts with the family, PPI will always assist families - everybody in the world has a mother and a father, and peace is very important for all.

Food waste is an enormous world problem. In the U. S. about 40% of all food is wasted. At the same time, as many as 12% of American households live in food insecurity.

Young people between ages 15 and 24 have the highest rate of auto-related deaths.

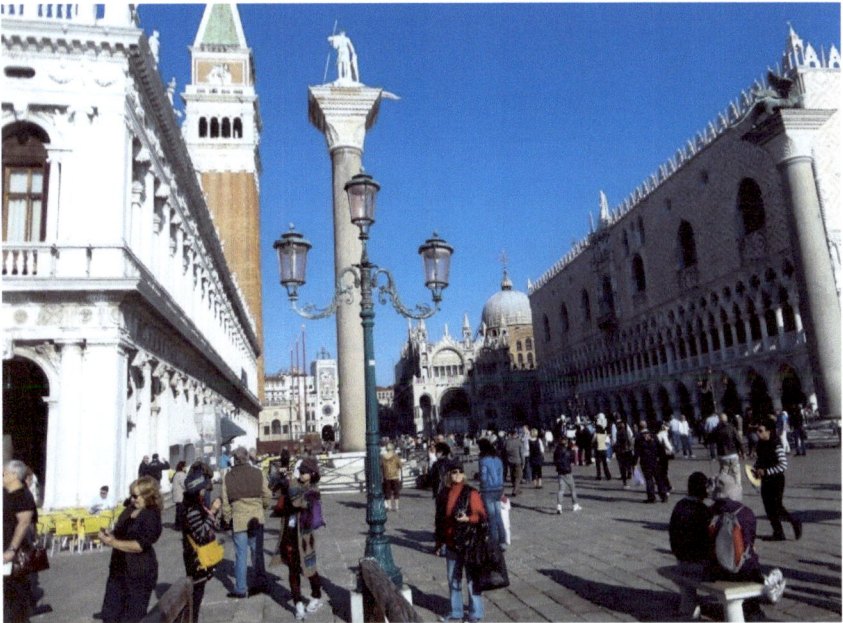

Venezia in 2012: from left: Libreria and Campanile, Torre dell'Orologio (back), San Theodore Column, Basilica (back), Palazzo Ducale, Lion of Venice Column (right).

Dispute resolution

Peace without dispute resolution is not possible - PPI will have a big role in helping with the dispute resolution everywhere.

People support the companies which decided to resolve any disputes by individual arbitration, and not by jury trial or class action.

New York (1624) in 2007: on 7th Avenue in Times Square, close to the W 43rd Street and to Times Square Tower (2004, 221 m, 47 fl.).

Informing people

It goes without saying that PPI must continuously inform people on its activities and results – and it must be short and clear.

Roma in 2011: Fontana di Trevi (1732 – 1762). Standing 26.3 m high and 49.15 m wide, it is located on Palazzo di Poli (1566).

Election assistance

Elections are important, and PPI will carefully support candidates who have a good record of supporting peace, freedom, health and prosperity – and, also, PPI will support civilized, polite and courteous elections.

Soon, an Election Commission of 110 representatives from the 10 regions and from the 100 sub-regions, elected separately for 5 years, will have to examine the qualifications of all the candidates for Advisers, and for other senior management positions. Unqualified candidates will be asked to improve their qualifications, and then to try again later.

It is important to refresh the management, and to bring new people to help the big family of 7.7 B people. The older generations, who performed well, will be retained in important roles, because experience and maturity count very much. At least two months before the retirement, they will kindly be asked to transfer their expertise to the younger generation. Even after retirement, they will occasionally be invited to share their expertise.

Good elections are essential for the future.

There has been a tendency to make elections conflict generating events, with lots of propaganda, false information, heavy donations, unpolite confrontations, bully fundraising, hostile political parties and organizations, unlimited power ambitions, etc.

This will be completely changed into clean, friendly elections, in which people choose between leaders with outstanding results, plus talent to lead people to peace and freedom, modesty, moderation, good character, friendliness, sharp mind, wisdom, good morals, and intense desire to help people – no campaigning, no publicity, no fundraising, no donations, no debates, no propaganda, no political parties, no advertising, or similar activities.

From Tokyo Skytree (2011, 634 m, at 350 m) looking south: Tobu Hotel Levant Tokyo (center) and other tall buildings near Sobu Main Line and Keiyo Road, tall buildings and Tokyo Denki University (a private university founded in 1907, and chartered as a university in 1949) near the Imperial Palace (right up), Tokyo Port in Bay of Tokyo (up center).

Membership cards

PPI will issue membership cards to its members - these cards will be useful for accessing buildings and events organized by PPI, and will be the base for the future Special Credit Cards, which will help everybody on Earth.

The special credit card (SCC) will be used to buy everything, to identify for voting, for census, for travel, for medical assistance, etc.

The current private credit cards will continue to work as usual.

The changes of the delimitations between regions, and also sub-regions, will be inputted on these cards, and no other work is needed.

Rome in 2011: Columna Traiani (113 AD) with a band (180 m) of carved reliefs, regarding Trajan's Dacian campaigns (101-102 and 105-106 AD). Left: Altare della Patria (1925).

No abuses

As always, it is expected to have strict discipline and no abuses in this preparation for peace, and the managers and all the people will pay attention to this.

When abuses happen, PPI will calmly assist people to correct the situation.

When somebody from government is abusive, special efforts from PPI will be needed.

In the world there are many reasoning errors, false belief, knowledge corruption, and impeded learning, and much effort is necessary to correct the issues.

People make errors all the time – including the error of blaming something else for their errors. Corrective actions are necessary.

Correcting errors is a permanent duty for everybody - Darwin (circa 140 years ago) said "To kill an error is as good a service as, and sometimes even better than, the establishing of a new truth or fact."

Special attention will be given by Advisors to avoid abuses and wrong interpretations of the rules. All assistants (doctors, mathematicians, CEOs, engineers and teachers) will closely monitor all activities, to avoid abuses and wrong interpretations of the rules.

This requirement of not having abuses is demanding – but this is a general job, not only for Government, but for everybody, as part of the big family, we just don't need abuses.

The abuse, in some places, of confiscating the land by some government bureaucrats will be eliminated – the land belongs to the people, not the government.

The abuse, in some places, of having trains, airplanes, and others making unhealthy noises, with the government support, will be eliminated – peoples' health has always priority.

The abuse, in some places, of having to change the clocks twice a year will be eliminated – only the normal local time zones will be used.

If abuses are observed, they will be immediately reported to the Government, and corrected, in general, by the People Assistance Department, which will have personnel, including medical assistants, to analyze and promptly solve the abuses.

Washington (1790) in 2007: Washington Monument (1848-1885, 169 m, 43 ha), National Mall, 700 m south of the White House.

Mediation

Everything under the Sun needs mediation from time to time - and PPI definitively will help, mediation and conciliation being closely related to peace.

Tokyo: on a street 75 m east of Kanda Myojin Shrine (744), a Shinto shrine located in Chiyoda (Nihonbashi).

Boston Harbor (1614, 130 km^2): Rowes Wharf (1987; in 1666 was a battery, in 1764 John Rowe built the first wharf): the stern (rear) of Clipper Stad Amsterdam (2000, 76 m x 10.5 m x 4.8 m x 46.5 m (the mainmast), sailing speed 17 knots (31.5 km/h), 31 sails, sail area 2200 m^2, 14 cabins (2 beds) for tourists, tonnage 723 BRT (Brotto Registered Tonnage, 2000 m^3), weight 1038 MT (Metric Tons) moored here, with the poop deck and mizzenmast visible.

People moving assistance

When people move from one place to another, PPI will be ready to assist - especially for families with children, and for elderly, who need to integrate in the new neighborhood.

People are something sacred for people.

The enemies of the people on Earth are not other people, but viruses, microbes, bad bacteria and hundreds of deadly illnesses – all people on Earth will work together against these real enemies for all of us.

USA: Heavy winter near Boston, in mid February 2014.

Cooperation

People need to cooperate, in order to maintain peace, and PPI will be there to help.

People of course can petition the small Word Government, and can change it anytime, if it does not perform as expected.

Inside Tokyo Skytree (2011, 634 m): a mural painting of the Skytree from above (left, with Sumidagawa River), and of the Skytree from across the Sumidagawa River (right

Prevention of accidents

Accidents always create stress and difficult situations - PPI will have useful information and techniques for prevention of accidents.

New York (1624) in 2007: on Broadway, close to Times Square, and to Times Square Tower (2004, 221 m, 47 floors

From Tokyo Skytree (2011, 634 m, at 450 m) looking north-east, Arakawa river (up horizontal), shadows of Skytree (down center) and of Tokyo Solamachi tower (down right), Tobu Skytree Line and Keisei Oshiage Line (center-right vertical), Kinegawabashi Bridge (up center right), Keisei Oshiage Line Bridge (up center), Yotsugibashi Bridges (up center left).

Commerce

Commerce is a necessity and a stimulant of peace - therefore it will be promoted and encouraged by PPI.

In one country, with one market, the commerce between the people on Earth will be free of taxes, tariffs, duties, etc. – plenty of opportunities for everybody.

Venezia in 2012: the south façade and a part of the east façade of Palazzo Ducale (1420, 152 m, Doge's Palace), which is situated on the south-east corner of Piazza San Marco (left).

Jobs

Good civilian jobs create a peaceful atmosphere, and PPI will be most interested to help.

Kindness is a requirement for everybody.
Seneca (circa 1,960 years ago) said "Wherever there is a human being, there is an opportunity for a kindness."
This is a fundamental idea which must be constantly applied

Vatican in 2011: St. Peter's Square (1667), the north-east colonnades (left), the Egyptian obelisk (2400 BC) and Bernini's fountain (1675, right).

Retirement

In retirement people are eager to have tranquility and peace – this is very important for PPI to have in mind, and to help.

New York (1624) in 2007: on 42nd street, close to 8th Avenue, inside a tall building, three sculptures of people waiting at a door.

Rural preparation for peace

Contacts with farmers, and others from the rural area, will be established by e-mails, video, phone, fax, letters and direct visits – it is an important factor in the preparation for peace.

Finland, Helsinki in 2013: commercial buildings south (left) and west (center) of Helsinki Central Railway Station (1907 – 1914).

Refugees from disasters

Flooding, hurricanes, earthquakes, volcanos, and other natural disasters create sometimes serious refugees' problems - PPI will be there to help and to keep the peace.

New York (1624) in 2007: on Broadway, between 50th and 51st Streets.

Peaceful relations at work

At work often appear stressful conflicts - they must be properly managed in order to restore harmony, and PPI will be ready to assist, when needed.

Self-discipline is a strict requirement for everybody.

All conflicts must not only be quickly resolved, but they must be transformed in friendships. This is very important for long term stability.

The medical personnel and others will work diligently to make sure that disputes are resolved, and then a friendship is developed. Only in this way the situation will become stable.

People want peace, freedom, health, friendship and prosperity, therefore conflicts should be quickly resolved, and then the corrective medical treatment will include the transformation of hostility and aggressiveness into harmony and friendship

Tokyo by night, with top brands advertisements in the famous Ginza District, east of the Imperial Palace.

Land disputes

Land disputes are the oldest and most frequent cause of serious conflicts - they require most attention – PPI will allocate resources to assist people to maintain peace.

Sometimes fences are needed - good fences make good neighbors.

Roma in 2011: Fontana del Tritone (Gian Lorenzo Bernini, 1642) in Piazza Barberini, with a text by Ovidius (43 BC – 17 AD

Water

Access to water is a burning issue in many places - good solutions must be found – PPI will carefully address these problems, to keep peace.

The sewer also must be working well, otherwise there is conflict – PPI will always work for peace.

Water purification and recycling is an essential world project.

Venezia in 2012: Palazzo Giustinian-Lolin (left) and a lovely palazzino on the north bank, near Ponte dell'Accademia, 870 m west of Piazza San Marco.

Religious activity

Much care is needed for religious activities.

Fortunately, many religious activities are very peaceful, and help preparing for peace. Those which are not so peaceful will need special attention, and PPI will help accordingly.

The religion will be free, and is expected not to interfere with activities of the Advisors, and actually should help people.

Italy, Rome, Vatican, Piazza San Pietro (1667, by Gian Lorenzo Bernini): Basilica di San Pietro (1506, center back), granite fountain by Carlo Maderno (1614, center, north side of piazza).

Tokyo Fish Market, near Shin-Ohashi Dori, Harumi Dori and No. 12 Oedo Line, 6 km south of Tokyo Imperial Palace

Sport

Occasionally, sport events become violent - this needs to be addressed, and PPI will play a role in maintaining the peace.

Paris in 2013: left: Atelier Brancusi (Constantin Brancusi, sculptor, 1876–1957), Musée national d'art moderne, on Rue Rambuteau; right: Centre Georges Pompidou (1971–1977, the Beaubourg area).

Tourism

Tourism is really important in the preparation for peace.
PPI will actively support civilized tourism in all directions.

Italy, Roma: The south-west side of the Amphitheatrum Flavium (80 AD, Colosseum), built by Vespasian Flavius and his son Titus.

Beautification

Using peace related art and decorations for beautification will be really pleasant, and PPI will have plenty of ideas, and will help anytime.

USA, Boston (founded in 1630) in 2009: visiting tall ships from many countries, at the Boston Fish Pier (opened in 1915).

A large statue of Ieyasu Tokugawa (1543 – 1616), the founder and first Edo Shogun. The Tokugawa shogunate of Japan ruled from 1600 to 1868. The statue is in front of the east entrance of Edo-Tokyo Museum, and it was erected in 1994, to celebrate the opening of the museum. Ieyasu rides on the back of a huge turtle, which is the metaphor for "Slow and steady Wins The Race" concept, and describes Ieyasu's life. The First Edo Shogun holds in the left hand the falcon, ready to start falconry, which he loved.

Nobility

These days the royal families and their relatives are interested in peace - PPI will stay in touch with them to work together for peace.

Roma in 2011: Mausoleum of Hadrian (117-138, Castel Sant'Angelo, 135-139).

Medical personnel

The collaboration with the medical personnel will be very intense and friendly – PPI will always be hand in hand with the medical personnel, who work for peace day in day out. World Diabetes Day (November 14) helps raise awareness of diabetes, which is a growing epidemic. A new World Health Organization (WHO)-led study says majority of adolescents worldwide are not sufficiently physically active, putting their current and future health at risk.

Medical assistance is not one size fits all – each person needs a customized medical assistance.

All people transmit deepest condolences to everyone who has lost a loved one in this COVID-19 pandemic. With world medical efforts, the pandemic will shortly disappear.

All people must get the medical care they need, at home.

Many bad things are happening every day in the world, to the detriment of many people, because sick people are not under medical treatment

Patient-initiated and doctor-initiated visits, video, voice or e-mail sessions are very important for better health and for saving lives.

Led by engineers at George Washington University and Northwestern University, researchers have developed a new class of medical instruments to improve the diagnoses and treatments of cardiac diseases. They applied stretchable matrices of electrode sensors and actuators, along with temperature and pressure sensors, to a balloon catheter system for minimally invasive surgeries

Veterans

Veterans and other military related people do need some extra attention - PPI will have a separate section for them, because they need explanations why it is better to switch to a civilian job, and good civilian jobs will be found.

People can assemble peacefully only. If some disagree with a decision, they can always inform the government, which will respond in 3 days. The discussion will continue with calm and respect, until everything is clarified.

Japan in 2008: the north-east side of Kawaguchiko (Lake Kawaguchi, 6 km^2, 830 m elevation) with hotel Route Inn (left), 17 km north of Mount Fuji (3,776 m, 1707 last eruption).

Peaceful Terra

Peaceful community living is a priority - PPI will certainly be involved in many communities, to explain the benefits of preparing for peace.

Peace is the first priority – without peace not much can be done.

The Proposition 2 of the World Constitution has the title Peaceful Terra.

Roma in 2011: Palazzo Madama (1505, atop the ruins of the Thermae (64) Neronianae (37-68)), the home of Senate of Italy

5 - Other tasks

Home visits

PPI will have extensive home visits, especially for people with medical problems and elderly, to create a peace-oriented atmosphere.

Medical doctors and assistants will make regular home visits to all people, to keep them healthy, and to prevent illnesses.

3 March is World Hearing Day – all people join Noisy Planet, the World Health Organization and many others in improving healthy hearing – people ask for Hearing care for all! Screen. Rehabilitate. All noise producing equipment must be changed in quiet equipment, using advanced technology.
To better understand how we hear, scientists used X-ray crystallography and supercomputers to study tiny structures in our ears.

Police collaboration

Preparing for peace includes a strong collaboration with civilized and polite police, who must maintain order, stop aggressive people, take care of accidents, disasters, etc.

The police powers will be limited, and they will know and be friend with all the people in their jurisdiction – this is the key element of a civilized and peaceful Earth. If they notice a person with bad intentions, they immediately retain that person and call for a medical assistant (and other assistants, if necessary), to analyze and solve the issue very quickly.

Police will be people's friends everywhere, and they will always help people.

In order to prevent bad things, the police, doctors and their assistants will be in permanent contact with all the people, by visiting them, phone calls, e-mails, tele-videos, and mail, to keep everybody calm and happy.

From Tokyo Skytree (2011, 634 m, at 350 m) looking south-west, Sumida river with bridges Komagatabashi (center-right), Umayabashi (center-left) and Kumaebashi (left), Edo-Tokyo Museum (center left), Asakusa dori (street from left down to right up), tall buildings near Tokyo Imperial Palace (up left) and Shinjuku (up right), Sumida Ward Office building (center-right), Isesaki Line (right down).

Arms elimination

It is understood that a sustainable peace can be achieved by eliminating all the arms - PPI will continuously work on this important problem.

The determination of all people to have peace, freedom, good health, good education, harmony and prosperity for all, is growing every day.

Healthy planet means healthy people, no arms (which pollute everything), healthy land and healthy oceans (which are 71% of Earth's surface).

All the oceans will belong to some of the regions, therefore will be maintained by those regions, to be free of any piracy or other bad activity – World Police will help when necessary.

Arms will not exist anymore, and only the police will have some small arms. Those who want arms for hunting or sport, will borrow them from police stations, with proper documents, rules and payments.

All military units will become strong civilian organizations, working to improve the quality of life for everybody.

For practical reasons, the transition from the current imperfect situation to the much better Sustainable Peace and Prosperity Structure (SPPS) will be very smooth: first - all the countries remain as they are, and they will begin – for example on January 1st, 2021 - to negotiate total and complete disarmament, with the help of the United Nations, for 3 months. Then for 5 months will intensely work to eliminate all the arms – either transform them in peaceful tools, or destroy them. Then a continuous verification and monitoring will be implemented, the make sure that the world finally achieved complete disarmament forever!

Freedom goes hand in hand with responsibility.

From Tokyo Skytree (2011, 634 m, ground level, the broadcasting, restaurant, and observation tower located in Sumida, Tokyo. It became the tallest structure in Japan in 2010 and reached its full height of 634 m in March 2011, making it the tallest tower in the world, and the second tallest structure in the world. The tower opened to the public on 22 May 2012. Without antenna it is 495 m, top observation floor is at 451.2 m, and the second observation floor is at 350 m. It has 13 elevators.) looking south to a canal and houses near Asakusa Dori (street farther south).

World cooperation

Preparing for peace is a world effort, therefore world cooperation is necessary.

William Shakespeare – "One touch of nature makes the whole world kin."

From a political point of view, the people of the world will integrate all political parties in a World Popular Association for Peace, Freedom, Health, Education, Jobs, Harmony and Prosperity for All (WOPAPEFEHEJOHAPQA, or shortly WOPAP). When this WOPAP achieves its goal of implementing the World Constitution in a few short years, it will dissolve itself with great satisfaction, and all people will enjoy good, healthy and harmonious life.

Finland, Helsinki in 2013:to the south of the Railway Square there is the Ateneum (1887, a major museum of classical art).

Japan: Kaguraden (1636, a building for the Kagura ritual) in Nikkō (140 km north of Tokyo, 25 km west of Utsunomiya, the capital of Tochigi Prefecture) - a town at the entrance to Nikko National Park, in the mountains (600 m) of Tochigi Prefecture, most famous for Toshogu, Japan's most extravagantly decorated shrine, and the mausoleum of Tokugawa Ieyasu, the founder of the Tokugawa shogunate (1600).

Training

PPI will have a section dedicated to training employees and others for this preparation for peace.

The press will be free and responsible. It is expected not to call for war, violence, or similar destructive activities. People want peace, freedom, health, friendship and prosperity.

Roma in 2011: La Bocca della Verità is a Pavonazzo marble sculpture, from around 50 AD, located at the church of Santa Maria in Cosmedin.

Sendai Station. Sendai is about 300 km north-east of Tokyo, the largest city in the Tohoku Region and one of the country's fifteen largest cities, with approximately one million inhabitants. The modern city of Sendai, which is the capital city of Miyagi Prefecture, was founded around 1600 by Date Masamune, one of feudal Japan's most powerful lords. Many of Sendai's tourist attractions are related to Masamune and his family.

Young generation

The young generation being the future, PPI will permanently work with young people for peace.

International research teams are the future of research and development.

Rome in 2011: part of the wall of Forum Augustum (2 BC), near Via Cavour.

Qualified personnel

PPI will look for well qualified people in all fields, because peace is important for all.

Japan, Nikko, (140 km north of Tokyo, with 103 shrines and temples): Massha Mitomo-jinja Honden (1755, building enshrining Sukunabikona no Mikoto, part of the 23 structures of the Futarasan Shrine (1619)).

Prevention first

Preventing violence and other bad events requires intense working closely with police and others, and PPI will determine when a risky situation occurs, and rapidly intervene to calm down the situation.

Individual responsibility is very important for all people on Earth.

Tokyo in 2014: Sumou Museum (green), Edo-Tokyo Museum (right back), north of Keiyo Road and Sobu Main Line, west of Kiosumi Dori and Toei Oedo Line, 4 km north-east of Tokyo Imperial Palace.

Japan: a wind turbine 150 m west from the north-east entrance of the Inzai campus of Tokyo Denki University (a private university founded in 1907, and chartered as a university in 1949), 35 km north-east of Tokyo Imperial Palace, 24 km west of Narita International Airport

Education work

PPI will be in contact with all schools, universities and other educational institutions, in order to implement a preparation for peace program at different levels of education.

The International Day of Education is 24 January.

Freedom is a fundamental requirement on Earth.

The speech will be free and responsible. It is expected not to call for war, violence, or similar destructive activities. People want peace, freedom, health, friendship and prosperity.

Roma in 201: Center-left: Altare della Patria (1925). Center-right: Columna Traiani (113 AD) and Trajan's statue, viewed from the north sidewalk of Via dei Fori Imperiali.

World library

PPI will work hard to have a world library, with facilities in many places in the world.

Peace, pioneering spirit, freedom and hard work will be the base of Peaceful Terra.

Venezia in 2012: il Campanile (right) and the Basilica Cattedrale Patriarcale di San Marco (center-back) appear in their entire splendor. Basilica was completed around 1071, has a height of 43 m, and is the finest example of Byzantine and Italic Gothic architectures in the world.

Adult education for peace

Peace is important for any age, therefore adult education for preparing for peace has a high priority for PPI.

Humanity's future is very clear: peace, no arms, freedom, good health, good education, harmony and prosperity for all, with a very friendly and efficient world government, according to the Constitution of the World.

Inspectors will help the Government with the integrity and efficiency issues – always there are ways to improve the work.

Inspectors will give advice regarding integrity and efficiency, and will take corrective actions when necessary.

Japan: Matsushima (20 km north-east of Sendai, with a beautiful bay (back, looking south-east), dotted by pine clad islets (left back); it is the most scenic view of Japan). To the right: Matsushima Kaigan Japanese Railroad Station, 600 m, Zuiganji Zen Temple, 450 m, Godaido Temple, 50 m. To the left, Fukuurajima Island, accessible via a long bridge, 600 m. The map has the north towards left down. Right down it is the sign for Tsunami Evacuation: to the right to Zuiganji Zen Temple, 450 m.

Peace in fine arts and music

There is a long tradition of promoting peace through fine arts and music - this tradition will be continued and extended.

Venezia, San Michele in 2012: a view from Isola di San Michele, situated between Venezia to the south and Murano to the north.

France, Paris: Musée du Louvre (1793): a statue representing art, in front of Pavillion Richelieu. in Cour Napoléon (1803). The Louvre is located on the right bank of La Seine, in the 1st arrondissement, and has about 35,000 museum objects, exhibited over an area of 60,600 m². With more than 8 million visitors each year, the Louvre is the world's most visited museum. The museum is housed in the Palais du Louvre, originally built as a fortress around 1190 under Philip II of France (1165 – 1223, king 1179 – 1223).

Peace and global media

The global media, many times, is helpful - PPI will work to have all global media support this preparation for peace.

Global innovation hubs are connecting the world to innovation outcomes, leading technological transformation and economic development. Global innovation hubs are cities or metropolitan areas that can lead the flow of global innovation elements. The Global Innovation Hubs Index highlights the roles of scientific research, a vibrant economy, and an open environment for driving innovation.

Examples of global innovation hubs include Silicon Valley, Boston area, Tokyo, Shenzhen, Moscow, Berlin, London, Paris, Zurich, Seoul, Rome, New Delhi.

Tokyo: The Holy Resurrection Cathedral or Nikorai-do (1891, 1929), a Japanese Orthodox Church, on the hill at Kanda Surugadai, overlooking the Imperial Palace (1.5 km south-west).

Finland, Helsinki in 2013: the central part of the Ateneum (1885 - 1887, a major museum of classical art). Up a phrase in Latin: Concordia res parvae crescund (By unity small states flourish). The four caryatids represent architecture, painting, music and sculpting.

History of peace

Most history books are about war and conflicts, but insistent work will be done to create a solid history of peace.

Canada, Niagara Falls, in 2013: the American Falls (21-30 m drop, 290 m wide, center), and the Bridal Veil Falls (center-right, 21m drop), after Luna Island.

Sendai: a view of the east side of Atago-Kamisugi Dori, looking south-west towards the Sendai Railroad Station. Sendai is about 300 km north-east of Tokyo, the largest city in the Tohoku Region and one of the country's fifteen largest cities, with approximately one million inhabitants. The modern city of Sendai, which is the capital city of Miyagi Prefecture, was founded around 1600 by Date Masamune, one of feudal Japan's most powerful lords.

Scholarships

Peace scholarships are useful – PPI will have some, for the younger generation.

Each government department will have some reserves for special situations (natural disasters, big accidents), and the banks will also have good financial reserves.

All people will be encouraged to save some money in banks with 5% interest.

Japan in 2008: the northern side of Mount Fuji (right, 3,776 m, 1707 last eruption), seen from 17 km north in Kawaguchiko (Lake Kawaguchi, 6 km², 830 m elevation), 100 km south-west of Tokyo.

France, Paris: Musée du Louvre (1793): a statue representing science, in front of Pavillion Richelieu, in Cour Napoléon (1803). The Louvre is located on the right bank of La Seine, in the 1st arrondissement, and has about 35,000 museum objects, exhibited over an area of 60,600 m^2. With more than 8 millions of visitors each year, the Louvre is the world's most visited museum. The museum is housed in the Palais du Louvre, originally built as a fortress around 1190 under Philip II of France (1165 – 1223, king 1179 – 1223).

Science & technology for peace

We'll have intense applications of mathematics, science and technology in the preparation for peace.

14 March is π (Pi) Day.

Japan: a colorful touristic train near Kawaguchiko (Lake Kawaguchi, 6 km^2, 830 m elevation, 100 km south-west of Tokyo, 17 km north of Mt Fuji, 3776 m, 1707 last eruption.

Cyberspace and peace

Like many other important discoveries, the cyberspace was invented by academics for peaceful collaboration – PPI will make sure that it will be used only for peaceful collaboration.

Cybersecurity for all: all computers will have a place for the user's card – the user's card will have the information about the user, will be registered (for a small fee) with the local cyber-police (which will be connected to the world cyber-police), and the user's card will appear on all the computers contacted by that user and on user's e-mails. If something unfriendly comes from a computer, it's user card number will be given to the cyber-police, who will immediately contact the user.

UK, Oxford: Oriel College (1326, in the back: the east range of First quadrangle, with ornate portico in the center)).

A gorgeous classical bronze sculpture on a street in Sendai (1600, 300 km north-east of Tokyo, the largest city in the Tohoku Region and one of the country's fifteen largest cities, with about one million inhabitants. Sendai is the capital city of Miyagi Prefecture.

Economic development and peace

It is very important to work hard to transform all the economy to be for peace purposes, and thus to have a very robust development of good products for all people, like good infrastructure everywhere, roads, bridges, water, sewer, electricity, gas, transportation, etc. The transport industry's improvement will be among the world government's highest priorities. The key objectives include upgrading the transit infrastructure, building major logistic hubs and international trade corridors, designing reliable and safe modes of transportation, and optimizing management solutions. It is imperative to integrate innovative technology more actively, and use the private-public partnership mechanisms more extensively.

The correct inflation rate in the world in 2021 is over 7%, and increasing fast. The inflation includes CPI, weighted stock inflation, and weighted budget deficit inflation.
There are continued increases in the general level of prices of goods, services, stocks, as well as budget deficits. Because of this the world economy will have difficulties, and people are for good leadership to reduce inflation.

Fiscal responsibility is a first priority for all.

For economy it is clear that the free market economy, while not perfect, gives the best results, but all people will have the option to choose between friendly private services, and friendly government services. Independent assistants and monitors will make sure that there are no abuses. Sine qua non requirements for happiness are morality and free market.

Japan, Tokyo (1150), in 2008: in Shinjuku, Shinjuku Center Bldg. (223 m, 54 fl, 1979, left), Mode Gakuen Cocoon Tower (204 m, 50 fl, 2008, center-left), Keio Plaza Hotel North Tower (180 m, 47 fl, 1971, center-right).

Flowers on a street in Tokyo, in 2014, close to a pedestrian overpass, near Tokyo International Forum and Harumi dori, 1 km south-east of Tokyo Imperial Palace.

Public works for peace

Usually the public works are peace-oriented, and this will be extended for all public works.

Boston Harbor (1614, 130 km^2): east of Rowes Wharf bldg. (1987; in 1666 was a battery, in 1764 John Rowe built the first wharf).

Risk analysis

There is always some risk in all activities, and a mathematical risk analysis is useful to eliminate possible conflicts.

Japan: a building with a teaching auditorium, 100 m west from the north-east entrance of the Inzai campus of Tokyo Denki University (a private university founded in 1907, and chartered as a university in 1949), 35 km north-east of Tokyo Imperial Palace, 24 km west of Narita International Airport.

Artificial Intelligence (AI) and peace

AI was created by academics for peaceful applications, and all people insist to remain only this way. AI technologies make it possible to get rid of the inertia and slowness of the bureaucratic machine, and to radically increase transparency and efficiency of administrative procedures. AI has capabilities to solve the problems of each person, and ultimately to change the quality of the entire system of public administration. AI can help to have comfortable and safe cities, accessible and high-quality healthcare and education, modern logistics and a reliable transportation system, exploration of space and the world ocean, sustainable and balanced development, the growing quality of life and new opportunities for all people.

AI and machine learning (ML), if not used for war and death, will improve medicine by making diagnosis and treatment more accessible and more effective for all.

Artificial intelligence must be used for the benefit of all people, not for killing people.

Japan: a beautiful bonsai tree on the north-east side of the Lake Kawaguchi (Kawaguchiko, 6 km², 830 m elevation), 100 km south-west of Tokyo, 17 km north of Mt Fuji (3,776 m, 1707 last eruption).

Peace research

Peace does not mean only no war - peace also includes harmony, friendship and prosperity – research is needed to develop these areas.

Examples:
Researchers at the National Institute of Standards and Technology have developed a method of added manufacturing gels that has the potential to create complex structures with nanometer-scale precision, leading to the development of soft medical devices that can be inserted into the human body.

Researchers led by a University of Houston engineer have reported the development of a cardiac patch made from fully rubbery electronics that can be placed directly on the heart to collect electrophysiological activity, temperature, heartbeat, and other indicators, all at the same time

Sensors that monitor a patient during medical procedures can be expensive, uncomfortable, even dangerous. An international research team has designed a highly sensitive, flexible gas sensor that can be implanted in the body and, when no longer needed, safely biodegrades into materials absorbed by the body.

Peaceful nuclear energy use

It is nothing wrong with peaceful nuclear energy use - and, at the same time, the elimination of all nuclear arms is a very high priority.

Ronald Reagan, State of the Union Address, 1984: "A nuclear war cannot be won and must never be fought. The only value, in our two nations possessing nuclear weapons, is to make sure they will never be used. But then would it not be better to do away with them entirely."

Lido di Venezia in 2012: the sandy beach by the Adriatic Sea, near Granviale Santa Maria Elisabetta.

World resources for peace

It is very important to have all the world resources used for peaceful purposes only.

The purpose for all people on Earth is to be healthy, to live in peace, freedom and harmony, to be prosperous, and to prepare to expand to the Moon, asteroids, Mars, and other places in the Universe, which can support life.

Washington, D.C. (1790) in 2007: a vending cart near the east side of the Smithsonian Institution Building (1849-1855), on Jefferson Drive SW, close to 7th Street SW.

Broadcasting for peace

Broadcasting for peace will be very useful, and it will be achieved as soon as possible.

From Tokyo Skytree (2011, 634 m, at 350 m) looking north-west, Sumida river with a bridge between Bokutei dori (route 461, center right) and Taitou Riverside Sports Center (center left).

Space exploration

Space exploration was always peaceful - and people want to remain this way – nobody wants to have nuclear bombs over their heads!

Paris in 2013: the east façade of the Grand Palais des Champs-Élysées (1900), the main entrance (left), on Av. Winston Churchill.

Ten regions

They are important for a sustainable peace, freedom and prosperity, therefore the preparation for peace should include a preparation for these ten regions.

Each region will have a pair of capitals plus an outside city, for better and more homogenous management (all will change every year; more details are in the annex book "World with One Country & its Ten Friendly Regions - Moving from 195 disagreeing countries, to 1 country with 10 collaborating regions"). For example, the first implementation will be:

Japan: decorations in a Japanese restaurant in Inzai, with a part of the restaurant being reserved for customers who prefer the Japanese tradition of seating on the floor (back).

R0 between meridians 0 and 15⁰ E, capitals: Bern (Switzerland), Libreville (Gabon), and Oxford (UK).

R1: 15⁰ E - 30⁰ E, Warsaw (Poland), Pretoria (South Africa) and Miami (FL, USA).

R2: 30⁰ E - 45⁰ E, Moscow (Russia), Cairo (Egypt), and Grenoble (France).

R3: 45⁰ E - 75⁰ E, Astana (Kazakhstan), Karachi (Pakistan), and Montpellier (France).

R4: 75⁰ E - 85⁰ E, New Delhi (India), Novosibirsk (Russia), and Magdeburg (Germany).

R5: 85⁰ E - 100⁰ E, Krasnoyarsk (Russia), Urumqi (China), and Avignon (France).

R6: 100⁰ E - 115⁰ E, Jakarta (Indonesia), Beijing (China), and Neuchâtel (Switzerland).

R7: 115⁰ E - 180⁰, Tokyo (Japan), Sydney (Australia), and Malmö (Sweden).

R8: 180⁰ - 70⁰ Washington (USA), Mexico City (Mexico), and Bellinzona (Switzerland).

R9: 70⁰ W – 0 Halifax (Canada), Brasilia (Brazil), and Biel (Switzerland).

Each of the 10 regions will be divided by meridians in 10 sub-regions S00,   , S99, each with about 77 M people.

Then each of the 100 sub-regions will be divided in 10 districts.

Meridians are easy to use, impartial, helpful for people with telework

Two capitals for each sub-region?

In Region R0: from Paris (France) to N'Djamena (Chad)

- The sub-region R00 will have the capitals Paris (France) and Niamey (Niger) – assistance from Magdeburg (Germany).
- The sub-region R01 will have the capitals Brussels (Belgium) and Porto-Novo (Benin) - assistance from Toronto (Canada).
- The sub-region R02 will have the capitals Amsterdam (Netherlands) and Algiers (Algeria) - assistance from Graz (Austria).
- The sub-region R03 will have the capitals Luxembourg (Luxembourg) and Sao Tome (Sao Tome and Principe) - assistance from Adelaide (Australia).
- The sub-region R04 will have the capitals of Abuja (Nigeria) and Bochum (Germany) - assistance from Nikko (Japan).
- The sub-region R05 will have the capitals Malabo (Equatorial Guinea), and Zürich (Switzerland) - assistance from Leeds (UK).
- The sub-region R06 will have the capitals Oslo (Norway) and Tunis (Tunisia) - assistance from Sheffield (UK).
- The sub-region R07 will have the capitals Roma (Italy) and Luanda (Angola) - assistance from Yamagata (Japan).
- The sub-region R08 will have the capitals in Berlin (Germany) and Tripoli (Libya) - assistance from New York (USA).
- The sub-region R09 will have the capitals Prague (Czech Republic) and N'Djamena (Chad) - assistance from Brisbane (Australia).

In Region R1: from Zagreb (Croatia) to Bujumbura (Burundi)

- The sub-region R10 will have the capitals in Zagreb (Croatia) and Brazzaville (Congo) - assistance from Nantes (France).
- The sub-region R11 will have the capitals in Vienna (Austria), Windhoek (Namibia) - assistance from Bilbao (Spain).
- The sub-region R12 will have the capitals in Stockholm (Sweden), Bangui (Central African Republic) - assistance from Florence (Italy).
- The sub-region R13 will have the capitals in Budapest (Hungary), Rundu (Namibia) - assistance from Monaco (Monaco).
- The sub-region R14 will have the capitals in Belgrade (Serbia), Kananga (Democratic Republic of Congo) - assistance from Liverpool (UK).
- The sub-region R15 will have the capitals in Athens (Greece), Mongu (Zambia) - assistance from Los Angeles (CA, USA).
- The sub-region R16 will have the capitals in Helsinki (Finland) and Kolwezi (Democratic Republic of the Congo) - assistance from Montreal (Canada).
- The sub-region R17 will have the capitals in Bucharest (Romania) and Gaborone (Botswana) - assistance from Philadelphia (PA, USA).
- The sub-region R18 will have the capitals in Minsk (Belarus) and Maseru (Lesotho) - assistance from Orleans (France).
- The sub-region R19 will have the capitals in Chisinau (Republic of Moldova) and Bujumbura (Burundi) - assistance from Hamburg (Germany).

In Region R2: from Kiev (Ukraine) to Baghdad (Iraq)

- The sub-region R20 will have the capitals in Kiev (Ukraine) and Kigali (Rwanda) - assistance from Ottawa (Canada).
- The sub-region R21 will have the capitals in Ankara (Turkey) and Khartoum (Sudan) - assistance from Salzburg (Austria).
- The sub-region R22 will have the capitals in Lilongwe (Malawi) and Nicosia (Cyprus) - assistance from Dallas (TX, USA).
- The sub-region R23 will have the capitals in Jerusalem (Israel) and Dodoma (Tanzania) - assistance from Strasbourg (France).
- The sub-region R24 will have the capitals in Damascus (Syria) and Nairobi (Kenya) - assistance from Stuttgart (Germany).
- The sub-region R25 will have the capitals in Krasnodar (Russia) and Addis Ababa (Ethiopia) - assistance from Marseille (France).
- The sub-region R26 will have the capitals in Rostov-on-Don (Russia) and Asmara (Eritrea) - assistance from Leipzig (Germany).
- The sub-region R27 will have the capitals in Stavropol (Russia) and Djibouti (Djibouti) - assistance from Zürich (Switzerland).
- The sub-region R28 will have the capitals in Mosul (Iraq) and Moroni (Comoros) - assistance from Linz (Austria).
- The sub-region R29 will have the capitals in Yerevan (Armenia) and Baghdad (Iraq) - assistance from Göttingen (Germany).

In Region R3: from Riyadh (Saudi Arabia) to Malé (Maldives)

- The sub-region R30 will have the capitals in Riyadh (Saudi Arabia) and Mogadishu (Somalia) - assistance from Bonn (Germany).
- The sub-region R31 will have the capitals in Baku (Azerbaijan) and Antananarivo (Madagascar) - assistance from Le Mans (France).
- The sub-region R32 will have the capitals in Oral (Kazakhstan) and Tehran (Iran) - assistance from Pisa (Italy).
- The sub-region R33 will have the capitals in Ashgabat (Turkmenistan) and Abu Dhabi (United Arab Emirates) - assistance from Wolfsburg (Germany).
- The sub-region R34 will have the capitals in Magnitogorsk (Russia) and Muscat (Oman) - assistance from Toulouse (France).
- The sub-region R35 will have the capitals in Chelyabinsk (Russia) and Herat (Afghanistan) - assistance from Basel (Switzerland).
- The sub-region R36 will have the capitals in Tyumen (Russia) and Kandahar (Afghanistan) - assistance from Nagoya (Japan).
- The sub-region R37 will have the capitals in Dushanbe (Tajikistan) and Labytnangi (Russia) - assistance from Limoges (France).
- The sub-region R38 will have the capitals in Tashkent (Uzbekistan) and Kabul (Afghanistan) - assistance from Rostock (Germany).
- The sub-region R39 will have the capitals in Islamabad (Pakistan) and Malé (Maldives) - assistance from La Rochelle (France).

In Region R4: from Bishkek (Kyrgyzstan) to Brahmapur (India)

- The sub-region R40 will have the capitals in Bishkek (Kyrgyzstan) and Jaipur (India) - assistance from Osaka (Japan).
- The sub-region R41 will have the capitals in Akola (India) and Kashgar (China) - assistance from Genoa (Italy).
- The sub-region R42 will have the capitals in Almaty (Kazakhstan) and Coimbatore (India) - assistance from Perth (Australia).
- The sub-region R43 will have the capitals in Kuybyshev (Russia) and Agra (India) - assistance from Fukuoka (Japan).
- The sub-region R44 will have the capitals in Vertikos (Russia) and Nagpur (India) - assistance from Coral Bay (Australia).
- The sub-region R45 will have the capitals in Chennai (India) and Colombo (Sri Lanka) - assistance from Sapporo (Japan).
- The sub-region R46 will have the capitals in Lucknow (India) and Fedosikha (Russia) - assistance from Niigata (Japan).
- The sub-region R47 will have the capitals in Bilaspur (India) and Kolpashevo (Russia) - assistance from Albany (Australia).
- The sub-region R48 will have the capitals in Visakhapatnam (India) and Barnaul (Russia) - assistance from Hiroshima (Japan).
- The sub-region R49 will have the capitals in Brahmapur (India) and Tomsk (Russia) - assistance from Yokohama (Japan).

In Region R5: from Kathmandu (Nepal) to Dehong (China)

- The sub-region R50 will have the capitals in Kathmandu (Nepal) and Patna (India) - assistance from Kobe (Japan).
- The sub-region R51 will have the capitals in Bayingol (China) and Novokuznetsk (Russia) - assistance from Vichy (France).
- The sub-region R52 will have the capitals in Thimphu (Bhutan) and Dhaka (Bangladesh) - assistance from Jena (Germany).
- The sub-region R53 will have the capitals in Lhasa (China) and Achinsk (Russia) - assistance from Reims (France).
- The sub-region R54 will have the capitals in Abakan (Russia) and Kumul (China) - assistance from Fribourg (Switzerland).
- The sub-region R55 will have the capitals in Kyzyl (Russia) and Dibrugarh (India) - assistance from Denmark (Australia).
- The sub-region R56 will have the capitals in Bassein (Myanmar) and Tinsukia (India) - assistance from Chiba (Japan).
- The sub-region R57 will have the capitals in Yushu City (China) and Tinskoy (Russia) - assistance from Klagenfurt (Austria).
- The sub-region R58 will have the capitals in Jiuquan (China) and Medan (Indonesia) - assistance from Lucerne (Switzerland).
- The sub-region R59 will have the capitals in Chiang Mai (Thailand) and Dehong (China) - assistance from Mulhouse (France).

In Region R6: from Bangkok (Thailand) to Chita (Russia)

- The sub-region R60 will have the capitals in Bangkok (Thailand) and Kuala Lumpur (Malaysia) - assistance from Besançon (France).
- The sub-region R61 will have the capitals in Vientiane (Laos) and Singapore – assistance from Freiburg im Breisgau (Germany).
- The sub-region R62 will have the capitals in Phnom Penh (Cambodia) and Irkutsk (Russia) – assistance from Baden (Switzerland).
- The sub-region R63 will have the capitals in Palembang (Indonesia), Hanoi (Vietnam) – assistance from Thun (Switzerland).
- The sub-region R64 will have the capitals in Ulan Bator (Mongolia) and Ulan-Ude (Russia) – assistance from Chaumont (France).
- The sub-region R65 will have the capitals in Cirebon (Indonesia) and Nanning (China) – assistance from Vaduz (Lichtenstein).
- The sub-region R66 will have the capitals in Pontianak (Indonesia) and Baotou (China) – assistance from Lugano (Switzerland).
- The sub-region R67 will have the capitals in Surakarta (Indonesia) and Yichang (China) – assistance from Thonon-les-Bain (France).
- The sub-region R68 will have the capitals in Surabaya (Indonesia) and Changsha (China) – assistance from Burgdorf (Switzerland).
- The sub-region R69 will have the capitals in Chita (Russia) and Hong Kong (China) – assistance from Colmar (France).

In Region R7: from Nanchang (China) to Melbourne (Australia)

- The sub-region R70 will have the capitals in Bandar Seri Begawan (Brunei Darussalam) and Nanchang (China) – assistance from Turku (Finland).
- The sub-region R71 will have the capitals in Krasnokamensk (Russia) and Jinan (China) – assistance from St. Gallen (Switzerland).
- The sub-region R72 will have the capitals in Baguio City (Philippines) and Hangzhou (China) – assistance from Dole (France).
- The sub-region R73 will have the capitals in Manila (Philippines) and Taipei (Taiwan, China) – assistance from Metz (France).
- The sub-region R74 will have the capitals in Kupang (Indonesia) and Shanghai (China) – assistance from Davos (Switzerland).
- The sub-region R75 will have the capitals in Pyongyang (North Korea) and Seoul (South Korea) – assistance from Versailles (France).
- The sub-region R76 will have the capitals in Vladivostok (Russia) and Busan (South Korea) – assistance from Innsbruck (Austria).
- The sub-region R77 will have the capitals in Kyoto (Japan) and Khabarovsk (Russia) – assistance from Germering (Germany).
- The sub-region R78 will have the capitals in Nagoya (Japan) and Komsomolsk-on-Amur (Russia) – assistance from Venice (Italy).
- The sub-region R79 will have the capitals in Sendai (Japan) and Melbourne (Australia) – assistance from St. Moritz (Switzerland).

東照宮 五重塔心柱特別公開

江戸と日光 新たなつながり

2014. 3. 30   0:12

Japan: a panel (showing that the altitude of the top of the nearby five-storied pagoda Gojunoto (1818) is the same with the height of Tokyo Skytree (2011), 634 m) in Nikkō (140 km north of Tokyo, 25 km west of Utsunomiya, the capital of Tochigi Prefecture) - a town at the entrance to Nikko National Park, in the mountains (600 m) of Tochigi Prefecture, most famous for Toshogu, Japan's most lavishly decorated shrine, and the mausoleum of Tokugawa Ieyasu, the founder of the Tokugawa shogunate (1600).

In Region R8: from Anchorage (Alaska, USA) to Lima (Peru)

- The sub-region R80 will have the capitals in Uelen (Russia) and Anchorage (Alaska, USA), – assistance from Zug (Switzerland).
- The sub-region R81 will have the capitals in Vancouver (Canada) and San Jose (CA, USA) – assistance from Odense (Denmark).
- The sub-region R82 will have the capitals in Vernon (Canada) and Los Angeles (CA, USA) – assistance from Amstetten (Austria).
- The sub-region R83 will have the capitals in Calgary (Canada) and Tijuana (Mexico) – assistance from Chur (Switzerland).
- The sub-region R84 will have the capitals in Hermosillo (Mexico) and Tucson (AR, USA) – assistance from Bergen (Norway).
- The sub-region R85 will have the capitals in Chihuahua (Mexico) and Regina (Canada) – assistance from Gothenburg (Sweden).
- The sub-region R86 will have the capitals in San Luis Potosi City (Mexico) and Winnipeg (Canada) – assistance from Yverdon-les-Bains (Switzerland).
- The sub-region R87 will have the capitals in Tulsa (OK, USA) and Veracruz (Mexico) – assistance from Bregenz (Austria).
- The sub-region R88 will have the capitals in Memphis (TN, USA) and San José (Costa Rica) – assistance from Uppsala (Sweden).
- The sub-region R89 will have the capitals in Lima (Peru) and Boston (MA, USA) – assistance from Tampere (Finland).

In Region R9: from La Paz (Bolivia) to London (United Kingdom)

- The sub-region R90 will have the capitals in La Paz (Bolivia) and Bangor (Maine, USA) – assistance from Aosta (Italy).
- The sub-region R91 will have the capitals in Caracas (Venezuela) and Road Town (British Virgin Islands) – assistance from Obergoms (Switzerland).
- The sub-region R92 will have the capitals in Buenos Aires (Argentina) and Fort-de-France (Martinique) – assistance from Freudenstadt (Germany).
- The sub-region R93 will have the capitals in Asuncion (Paraguay) and Montevideo (Uruguay) – assistance from Winterthur (Switzerland).
- The sub-region R94 will have the capitals in Cayenne (French Guiana), St. John's (Canada) – assistance from Novara (Italy).
- The sub-region R95 will have the capitals in Rio de Janeiro (Brazil) and Dakar (Senegal) – assistance from Toyama (Japan).
- The sub-region R96 will have the capitals in Freetown (Sierra Leone) and Lisbon (Portugal) – assistance from Kawasaki (Japan).
- The sub-region R97 will have the capitals in Bamako (Mali) and Athlone (Ireland) – assistance from Ulm (Germany).
- The sub-region R98 will have the capitals in Yamoussoukro (Cote d'Ivoire) and Madrid (Spain) – assistance from Okayama (Japan).
- The sub-region R99 will have the capitals in Ouagadougou (Burkina Faso) and London (United Kingdom) - assistance from Vaasa (Finland).

World government

- The World Government will be limited to:
1) the Office of the Honorific Observer (less than 10 employees),
2) the Office of the top ten Advisors (less than 100 employees), and
3) 7 small departments:

- Tax Department

- Treasury

- People Assistance Department

- Medical Department

- Police

- Education Department

- Science & Technology Department

Peaceful Terra, with its family of over 7.7 B people, will have four levels of world management:

Level 1 Management: 1,000 L1 friendly managers, for the 1,000 districts, who will supervise and assist the mayors and town managers from their district, for a total of about 7,700,000 people in each district.

Level 2 Management: 100 L2 friendly managers, for the 100 sub-regions, who will supervise and assist the 10 L1 managers of the 10 districts of each sub-region, for a total of about 77,000,000 people for each sub-region.

Level 3 Management: Ten L3 friendly managers for the 10 regions, who will supervise and assist the 10 L2 managers of the 10 sub-regions of each region, for a total of about 770,000,000 people for each region.

Level 4 Management: very friendly 10 Advisers of the world, who will supervise and assist the 10 L3 managers of the 10 regions of the Earth, for a total of about 7,700,000,000 people – all the people on Earth, happy citizens of Peaceful Terra.

All the employees in Government will respect Seneca's (circa 1,960 years ago) aphorism "To govern is to serve, not to rule", and Hippocrates' (over 2,400 years ago) aphorism "Make a habit of two things: to help; or at least to do no harm."

Naturally, somebody has to administer the world for people's benefit and for peace – for more details please see the book by Michael M. Dediu: "Friendly, Helpful & Smart World Management - Moving from bureaucracy to responsive world management"

It is important to learn to manage yourself effectively, and then to help people on your team and your organization manage themselves better — for the benefit of all people.

All levels of government will be highly mobile - changing of the capitals for the 10 regions, and for the 100 sub-regions, etc.

It is necessary to move the government close to the people, to be able to quickly solve the local problems.

The sinews of the World Government will be very strong and clear.

World Constitution

Please see "The Constitution of the World – Moving from many unsustainable constitutions, to just one Constitution of the World".

Another recommended book is "Our Future is Sustainable Peace and Prosperity – Moving from conflicts to harmony and peace"

The following are the main World Constitution subjects:

- all the rules – not more than 2,000, on maximum 1,000 pages - on our Earth will be established by the people and their elected Advisers.

- small World Government, with 7 small departments

- elections - every 20 months for one term only, based on exceptional results, no propaganda

- advisors' levels - minimum age 25 years, First Adviser for one month, by rotation

- The L4 very friendly 10 Advisers of the world will be located each in one the ten Regions R0, R1,…, R9. For example, in the beginning, for the first month (then changing every month), the ten Advisers of the world will be located:

- in R0: Barcelona (Spain)
- in R1: Benghazi (Libya)
- in R2: Addis Ababa (Ethiopia)
- in R3: Hyderabad (Pakistan)
- in R4: Bhopal (India)
- in R5: Mandalay (Myanmar)
- in R6: Nanchong (China)
- in R7: Khabarovsk (Russia)
- in R8: Houston (USA)
- in R9: Recife (Brazil)

- assistants - each Advisor, and each manager at all levels, will have 5 immediate assistants:
1) a mathematician for finance and all other calculations,

2) a medical doctor for keeping everybody healthy, calm, polite, friendly and optimist,
3) a CEO for good management,
4) an engineer for all practical projects, and
5) a teacher for education, training and related areas.

- administrators
- Honorific Word Observer - will be quietly elected by direct vote – starting, for example, 1st September 2022 - for only one 3 years term, with the main duty to observe that the top 10 Advisers efficiently perform their duties, and keep their words – if they don't, they will be changed.

- medical assistance, Specialized Medical Institutions for disorderly behavior
- people assistance services
- some police with small arms
- total disarmament
- no conflicts
- no war
- no military forces
- no arms
- no abuses
- freedom and responsibility
- people can assemble peacefully only
- census: A census will take place every 5 years – starting, let's say on October 1st, 2023 - and all the people will receive a special credit card (SCC), with their photo and other personal data.
- special credit card with photo and other personal data. The special credit card (SCC) will be used to buy everything, to identify for voting, for census, for travel, for medical assistance, etc.
- World Central Bank: The SCC will be issued by the World Central Bank, which will include all current central banks – starting, let's say on May 1st, 2023.
- new world currency
- budgets with surplus
- tax: 15% of income
- no borrowing
- 40 hours/week, compensation

- savings accounts for old age
- International standards
- Intellectual Property
- World Post Offices
- free commerce and collaboration
- common sense
- prevention of bad events first - if bad, then pay all expense and reimburse
- language and alphabet

The World Constitution Day is 6 March.

The objective of the World Constitution is simply to help all the people on Earth to live better, peacefully, free, healthy, and prosperous.   More precisely, the Constitution starts with 7 details about its objectives in Proposition 1:

Proposition 1. We, the People of the World

We, the People on this Earth, in order to
1.1 - completely eliminate war and any type of conflicts,
1.2 - have a peaceful and harmonious world,
1.3 - have freedom, dignity, good families and respect,
1.4 - have good health and good education,
1.5 - have a friendly atmosphere and prosperity,
1.6 – have the safety and wellbeing of all the people in the world as the highest priority,
1.7 – use the best peaceful results, experience and knowledge of all current countries,

establish this Constitution of the World.

The Constitution of the World is ready to come into force, and to be put into practice, for the benefit of all people on Earth, on 6 March 2020, and it is ready to remain into force, and enjoyed by all people, at least until 6 March 12020.

Good Leaders

For world leaders, constant uncertainty and unforeseen disruptions are very frequent – then people need to see good leadership style, decision-making, influence, and overall effectiveness.

People want world leaders who are business acumen, have joy, curiosity, an innate ability to make others feel welcome, a faith-based humility that constantly reminds them of their place the universe (it was not at its center), and makes them personalities which others want to follow.

Fortunately, there are such good leaders.

Japan: an ornate monument near Sukibe temple (1620) in Nikkō (140 km north of Tokyo, 25 km west of Utsunomiya, the capital of Tochigi Prefecture, 600 m altitude).

Conclusions

Now, pour la bon bouche, let's start with the children - if all the over 2 billions of children in the world will get a solid peace-oriented education (see Dediu's book at number 90 in bibliography: Our Future Depends on Good World Educations – Moving from frail education to solid education), our future will be in good hands!

The purpose of education is, simply, to give a solid peace-oriented foundation for a good, free, peaceful, healthy, productive and prosperous life.

The purpose for all over 7.7 billions of people on Terra is to be healthy, to live in peace, freedom and harmony, to be prosperous, and to prepare to expand to the Moon, asteroids, Mars, and other places in the Universe, which can support life.

First of all, people must have a good World Government, as described in Dediu's book "Friendly, Helpful & Smart World Management - Moving from bureaucracy to responsive world management". Then people will be able to:
- Reserve time for happiness
- Use robots and automated processes, work less, and spend more time with their families
- Use weekends like small vacations
- Prevent burnout
- Make civilized harmony everywhere an important issue
- Eliminate stress
- Help friends and colleagues
- Keep everybody relaxed, calm, friendly, patient, and happy.

No arms = real joy + prosperity!

Bibliography

"The Histories" by Polybius
"Discours de la Méthode" by René Descartes
"Meditationes de prima philosophia" by René Descartes
"Philosophiae Naturalis Principia Mathematica" by Isaac Newton
Chinese encyclopedia Gujin Tushu Jicheng (Imperial Enciclopaedia)
"Encyclopédie" by Jean-Baptiste le Rond d'Alembert and Denis Diderot
"Encyclopaedia Britannica" by over 4,400 contributors
"Encyclopedia Americana" by Francis Lieber
"Grand Larousse encyclopédique en 24 volumes" by Albert Ducrocq
Nobel Prize Organization
"The Cambridge History of Medicine", edited by Roy Porter
"Great Russian Encyclopedia" by Yury Osipov
"Encyclopedia of China"
"Enciclopedia Italiana di Scienze, Lettere ed Arti" (35 volume), by Giovanni Treccani
Concise Oxford Dictionary of Opera
"Allgemeine Encyclopädie der Wissenschaften und Künste" by Johann Samuel Ersch und Johann Gottfried Gruber
Grove Dictionary of Music and Musicians
"Gran Enciclopedia de España"
Other sources include: UPI, CNBC, AP, Nasdaq, Reuters, EDGAR, AFP, Recode, Europa Press, Bloomberg News, Fox News, USA, Deutsche Presse-Agentur, MSNBC, BBC, Australian Associated Press, Agência Brasil, The Canadian Press (La Presse Canadienne), Middle East News Agency, Baltic News Service, Suomen Tietotoimisto, Athens-Macedonian News Agency, Asian News International, Inter Press Service, Kyodo News, Notimex, Algemeen Nederlands Persbureau, AGERPRES, Newsis, Tidningarnas Telegrambyrå, Swiss Telegraphic Agency, Central News Agency, ANKA news agency, Agenzia Fides

Japan: the north side of Mount Fuji (3,776 m, 1707 last eruption) seen from Kawaguchiko (Lake Kawaguchi, 6 km², 830 m elevation, 100 km south-west of Tokyo, 17 km north of Mount Fuji), with a branch of a blossomed cherry.

Michael M. Dediu is also the author of these books (which can be found on Amazon.com):

1. Aphorisms and quotations – with examples and explanations
2. Axioms, aphorisms and quotations – with examples and explanations
3. 100 Great Personalities and their Quotations
4. Professor Petre P. Teodorescu – A Great Mathematician and Engineer
5. Professor Ioan Goia – A Dedicated Engineering Professor
6. Venice (Venezia) – a new perspective. A short presentation with photographs
7. La Serenissima (Venice) - a new photographic perspective. A short presentation with many photos
8. Grand Canal – Venice. A new photographic viewpoint. A short presentation with many photos
9. Piazza San Marco – Venice. A different photographic view. A short presentation with many photos
10. Roma (Rome) - La Città Eterna. A new photographic view. A short presentation with many photos
11. Why is Rome so Fascinating? A short presentation with many photos
12. Rome, Boston and Helsinki. A short photographic presentation
13. Rome and Tokyo – two captivating cities. A short photographic presentation
14. Beautiful Places on Earth – A new photographic presentation
15. From Niagara Falls to Mount Fuji via Rome - A novel photographic presentation
16. From the USA and Canada to Italy and Japan - A fresh photographic presentation
17. Paris – Why So Many Call This City Mon Amour - A lovely photographic presentation
18. The City of Light – Paris (La Ville-Lumière) - A kaleidoscopic photographic presentation
19. Paris (Lutetia Parisiorum) – the romance capital of the world - A kaleidoscopic photographic view
20. Paris and Tokyo – a joyful photographic presentation. With a preamble about the Universe

France, Paris: Tour Eiffel (1889, 324 m, 279 m 3rd level, looking north-west): Tour Eiffel shadow (center-right down), Pont d'Iéna over Seine (center down), Av. de New York (on the north side of Seine), Jardin du Trocadéro (center-down), Chaillot Palace (middle), Av. du Président Wilson (green, horizontal, middle), Allée. Maria Callas (center to left up), Bois de Boulogne (green up), tall buildings in Courbevoie near Seine (up center, 4.5 km away).

21. From USA to Japan via Canada – A cheerful photographic documentary

22. 200 Wonderful Places, In The Last 50 Years – A personal photographic documentary

23. Must see places in USA and Japan - A kaleidoscopic photographic documentary

24. Grandeurs of the World - A kaleidoscopic photographic documentary

25. Corneliu Leu – writer on the same wavelength as Mark Twain. An American viewpoint

26. From Berkeley to Pompeii via Rome – A kaleidoscopic photographic documentary

27. From America to Europe via Japan - A kaleidoscopic photographic documentary

28. Discover America and Japan - A photographic documentary

29. J. R. Lucas – philosopher on a creative parallel with Plato, An American viewpoint

30. From America to Switzerland via France - A photographic documentary

31. From Bretton Woods to New York via Cape Cod - A photographic documentary

32. Splendid Places on the Atlantic Coast of the U. S. A. - A photographic documentary

33. Fourteen nice Cities on three Continents - A photographic documentary

34. 17 Picturesque Cities on the World Map - A photographic documentary

35. Unforgettable Places from Four Continents including Trump buildings - A photographic documentary

36. Dediu Newsletter, Volume 1, Number 1, 6 December 2016 – Monthly news, review, comments and suggestions for a better and wiser world

37. Dediu Newsletter, Volume 1, Number 2, 6 January 2017 (available at www.derc.com).

38. Dediu Newsletter, Volume 1, Number 3, 6 February 2017 (available at www.derc.com).

39. London and Greenwich, A photographic documentary

UK, London: On Broad Ct looking northeast, off Bow Street to the northeast, 50 m north of the Royal Opera House at Covent Garden (1732, 1808, 1858, 1999, capacity 2,256; in 1734, Covent Garden presented its first ballet, Pygmalion), the bronze statue Young Dancer, by the Italian-born (in Mestre, near Venice, in 1921) British sculptor Enzo Plazzotta (1921-1981 (age 60)). To the right up, five red telephone boxes, at 5 Broad Ct, a tourist attraction.

40. Dediu Newsletter, Volume 1, Number 4, 6 March 2017 (available also at www.derc.com).

41. Dediu Newsletter, Volume 1, Number 5, 6 April 2017 (available also at www.derc.com).

42. Dediu Newsletter, Volume 1, Number 6, 6 May 2017 (available also at www.derc.com).

43. Dediu Newsletter, Volume 1, Number 7, 6 June 2017 (available also at www.derc.com).

44. London, Oxford and Cambridge, A photographic documentary

45. Dediu Newsletter, Volume 1, Number 8, 6 July 2017 (available also at www.derc.com).

46. Dediu Newsletter, Volume 1, Number 9, 6 August 2017 (available also at www.derc.com).

47. Dediu Newsletter, Volume 1, Number 10, 6 September 2017 (available also at www.derc.com).

48. Three Great Professors: President Woodrow Wilson, Historian Germán Arciniegas, Mathematician Gheorghe Vrănceanu, A chronological and photographic documentary

49. Dediu Newsletter, Volume 1, Number 11, 6 October 2017 (available also at www.derc.com).

50 Dediu Newsletter, Volume 1, Number 12, 6 November 2017 (available also at www.derc.com).

51 Dediu Newsletter, Volume 2, Number 1 (13), 6 December 2017 (available also at www.derc.com).

52 Two Great Leaders: Augustus and George Washington, A chronological and photographic documentary

53. Dediu Newsletter, Volume 2, Number 2 (14), 6 January 2018 (available also at www.derc.com).

54. Newton, Benjamin Franklin, and Gauss, A chronological and photographic documentary

55. Dediu Newsletter, Volume 2, Number 3 (15), 6 February 2018 (available also at www.derc.com).

56. 2017: World Top Events, But Many Little Known, A chronological and photographic documentary

57. Dediu Newsletter, Volume 2, Number 4 (16), 6 March 2018 (available also at www.derc.com).

58. Vergilius, Horatius, Ovidius, and Shakespeare, A chronological and photographic documentary.

UK, London: From Charing Cross Rd, looking southeast to the northwest part of the front part of the English Anglican church St Martin in the Fields (1724, at the northeast corner of Trafalgar Square in the City of Westminster, spire height 59 m, 12 bells, tenor bell weight 1,486 kg, excavations under found a grave from about 410 AD (Roman era), in 1222 there was a church here, in 1542 Henry VIII rebuilt the church, in 1606 James I enlarged the church). It is famous for its regular lunchtime and evening concerts; Academy of St Martin-in-the-Fields performs here, and many other ensembles.

59. Dediu Newsletter, Volume 2, Number 5 (17), 6 April 2018 (available also at www.derc.com).
60. Dediu Newsletter, Volume 2, Number 6 (18), 6 May 2018 (available also at www.derc.com).
61. Vivaldi, Bach, Mozart, and Verdi, A chronological and photographic documentary
62. Dediu Newsletter, Volume 2, Number 7 (19), 6 June 2018 (available also at www.derc.com).
63. Dediu Newsletter, Volume 2, Number 8 (20), 6 July 2018 (available also at www.derc.com).
64. Dediu Newsletter, Volume 2, Number 9 (21), 6 August 2018 (available also at www.derc.com).
65. World History, a new perspective - A chronological and photographic documentary.
66. World Humor History with over 100 Jokes, a new perspective - A chronological and photographic documentary
67. Dediu Newsletter, Vol 2, N 10 (22), 6 September 2018
68. Dediu Newsletter, Vol 2, N 11 (23), 6 October 2018
69. Da Vinci, Michelangelo, Rembrandt, Rodin - A chronological and photographic documentary
70. Dediu Newsletter, Vol 2, N 12 (24), 6 November 2018
71. Dediu Newsletter, Vol 3, N 1 (25), 6 December 2018
72. From Euclid to Edison - revelries in the last 75 years - A chronological and photographic documentary
73. Dediu Newsletter, Vol 3, N 2 (26), 6 January 2019
74. Socrates to Churchill - Aphorisms celebrated after 1960 - A chronological and photographic documentary
75. Dediu Newsletter Vol 3, Number 3 (27), 6 February 2019
76. Hippocrates to Fleming: Medicine History celebrated after 1943 - A chronological and photographic documentary
77. Dediu Newsletter, Volume 3, Number 4 (28), 6 March 2019
78. Dediu Newsletter, Volume 3, Number 5 (29), 6 April 2019
79. Archimedes to Ford: Invention History celebrated after 1943 - A chronological and photographic documentary
80. Dediu Newsletter, Volume 3, Number 6 (30), 6 May 2019
81. Sutherland to Pavarotti: Great Singers History - A chronological and photographic documentary
82. Dediu Newsletter, Volume 3, Number 7 (31), 6 June 2019
83. Dediu Newsletter, Volume 3, Number 8 (32), 6 July 2019

UK, Cambridge: From Trinity Ln, looking west through the entrance of Trinity Hall, (1350, by William Baterman (c 1298-1355, Bishop of Norwich between 1344 and 1355), a constituent college (the 5th oldest) of the University of Cambridge), to the Front Court and the entrance to the west building of the Front Court. To the northeast of Trinity Hall there is the separate Trinity College (1546, founder Henry VIII (1491-1547, reign 1509-1547), motto: Virtus Vera Nobilitas).

84. Augustus to Rockefeller: History of the Wealthiest People - A chronological and photographic documentary

85. Dediu Newsletter, Volume 3, Number 9 (33), 6 August 2019

86 – Pythagoras to Fermi: History of Science - A chronological and photographic documentary

87. Dediu Newsletter, Volume 3, Number 10 (34), 6 September 2019

88. Our Future is Sustainable Peace and Prosperity – Moving from conflicts to harmony and peace

89 - Dediu Newsletter, Volume 3, Number 11 (35), 6 October 2019 – World Monthly Report with News

90 – Our Future Depends on Good World Educations – Moving from frail education to solid education

91 - Dediu Newsletter, Volume 3, Number 12 (36), 6 November 2019 – World Monthly Report with News

92 – Friendly, Helpful & Smart World Management - Moving from bureaucracy to responsive world management

93 – If You Want Peace, Prepare for Peace! – Moving from preparation for war to preparation for peace

94 - Dediu Newsletter, Volume 4, Number 1 (37), 6 December 2019 – World Monthly Report with News and Suggestions for Sustainable Peace, Freedom and Prosperity

95 – World with One Country & its Ten Friendly Regions - Moving from 195 disagreeing countries, to 1 country with 10 collaborating regions

96 - Dediu Newsletter, Volume 4, Number 2 (38), 6 January 2020 – World Monthly Report with News and Suggestions for Sustainable Peace, Freedom and Prosperity

97 – After 10,000 Years of Conflicts, People want 10,000 Years of Harmony - Moving from continuous wars to stable peace

98 - Dediu Newsletter, Volume 4, Number 3 (39), 6 February 2020 – World Monthly Report with News and Suggestions for Sustainable Peace, Freedom and Prosperity

99 – The Constitution of the World – Moving from many unsustainable constitutions, to just one Constitution of the World

100 - Dediu Newsletter, Volume 4, Number 4 (40), 6 March 2020 – World Monthly Report with News and Suggestions for Sustainable Peace, Freedom and Prosperity

101 - Dediu Newsletter, Volume 4, Number 5 (41), 6 April 2020 – World Monthly Report

102 - Dediu Newsletter, Volume 4, Number 6 (42), 6 May 2020 – World Monthly Report

103 – World Constitution Implementation – Moving from violent changes, to smooth transition to the Constitution of the World

104 - Dediu Newsletter, Volume 4, Number 7 (43), 6 June 2020 – World Monthly Report

105 - Dediu Newsletter, Volume 4, Number 8 (44), 6 July 2020 – World Monthly Report

106 - It is getting truer and truer – we urgently need the World Constitution: Moving from anarchic changes, to balanced transition to the Constitution of the World

107 - Dediu Newsletter, Volume 4, Number 9 (45), 6 August 2020 – World Monthly Report

108 - World Constitution with Lovely Comments - Moving from many suboptimal constitutions to the much better Constitution of the World

109 - Dediu Newsletter, Volume 4, Number 10 (46), 6 September 2020 – World Monthly Report

110 – World Constitution with Questions & Answers – Moving from many obsolete constitutions to the much better Constitution of the World

111 - Dediu Newsletter, Volume 4, Number 11 (47), 6 October 2020 – World Monthly Report

112 - World Projects - Moving from minor projects to great projects for the World

113 - Dediu Newsletter, Volume 4, Number 12 (48), 6 November 2020 – World Monthly Report

114 - Dediu Newsletter, Volume 5, Number 1 (49), 6 December 2020 – World Monthly Report

115 - World Opportunities for All - Moving from few local jobs, to world opportunities for all

116 - Dediu Newsletter, Volume 5, Number 2 (50), 6 January 2021 – World Monthly Report

117 - Self-Managing World - Moving from local ruling top-down, to self-managing world

118 – We are all in the same space boat – Peaceful Terra; Moving from local fragile boats to the solid Peaceful Terra

119 - Dediu Newsletter, Volume 5, Number 3 (51), 6 February 2021
– World Monthly Report
120 - All people ask for Peace + Freedom = Prosperity, Moving
from local conflicts to world peace and freedom
121 - Dediu Newsletter, Volume 5, Number 4 (52), 6 March 2021 –
World Monthly Report

Mathematical Reviews: American Mathematical Society (AMS)
sent for review, over the years, 301 mathematical research papers
and books, to Michael M. Dediu, and his reviews were published in
the Mathematical Reviews of the AMS.

Boston Harbor (1614), Rowes Wharf (1987): the 3 masts of Clipper
Stad Amsterdam (left, 2000), yacht Odyssey (right).

Japan: a splendid sculpture of a young woman on the north-east part of Lake Kawaguchi (6 km², 830 m elevation, 100 km south-west of Tokyo, 17 km north of Mt Fuji, 3776 m), near route 137 and Kukuna Hotel (up back).

www.ingramcontent.com/pod-product-compliance
Lightning Source LLC
Chambersburg PA
CBHW041308210326
41599CB00003B/32